3 1994 01153 8508

SANTA ANA PUBLIC LIBRARY

D0820798

ANIMALS CAN BE SO HARD TO SEE

GREYSTONE BOOKS

DOUGLAS & McINTYRE PUBLISHING GROUP

VANCOUVER/TORONTO/NEW YORK

J 591.472 SWA
Swanson, Diane
Animals can be so hard to
see OCT 8 2002
$10.95
CENTRAL 31994011538508

CONTENTS

Nesting,

Tunneling,

Hiding,

Animals can be so hard to see.

I SPY, YOU SPY

Find who's nesting, who's tunneling, who's hiding.

...nesting...

Nesting in a thick bush,
A family is hidden.
The young birds stay safe at home
While parents go for food.

I SPY, YOU SPY

Find four little mouths—
open WIDE—in the nest.

3

...denning.......

Deep in a snowdrift,
A polar bear is denning.
While freezing winds whirl overhead,
It lies low—snug and warm.

I SPY, YOU SPY
Find snow that's been rubbed smooth by the polar bear's heavy head.

...disguising...

Brown on brown and speckles on speckles,
A gecko—disguised as a rock—
Hides as it hunts for bugs.

I SPY, YOU SPY

Find the gecko's l–o–n–g tail. It looks like part of the rock.

...tunneling....

8

Softly, on night feet,

A busy rat tunnels.

It nibbles and gnaws

Inside buildings and logs.

I SPY, YOU SPY

Find the rat's whiskers.
They help it feel its way
in the dark.

...mimicking...

White yucca moth on white yucca flower.

In color and shape,

It mimics the bloom.

I SPY, YOU SPY

Find which parts of the flower are most like the moth.

...burrowing...

Red foxes burrow to make homes for pups.
The dens they dig beneath big logs
Help keep pups out of sight.

I SPY, YOU SPY

Find flowers that can hide the foxes when they're outside the den.

...creeping......

Creeping behind screens of green bamboo,
A tiger waits and watches
For dinner to appear.

I SPY, YOU SPY

Find the tiger's stripes. They break up its shape, making it harder to see.

...hiding...........

Ocean fish hide in thick seaweed forests.
They weave through waving shadows
While searching for food.

I SPY, YOU SPY
Find five fish among the seaweed. Can you spot even more?

...blending.....

Silent, still, the ptarmigan (TAR-mi-guhn)
Rests upon the snow.
Its feathered coat—white and fluffy—
Blends with winter's cover.

I SPY, YOU SPY

Find two parts of the ptarmigan that are not the color of snow.

Nesting,
Tunneling,
Hiding,
Animals can be so

hard to see.

Points for Parents

 Birds of many species nest in shrubs and trees around the world. Most build their own nests, often using twigs and grass.

 Red foxes are wild dogs that have red, gray-brown, or silvery black coats. They're adaptable enough to live almost everywhere—except deserts and dense woods.

 Polar bears are huge mammals that live on islands and along coasts in countries around the Arctic Ocean.

 Tigers are big wild cats that roam woodlands and open forests in Asia. They stalk prey such as deer, antelopes, and wild pigs.

 Geckos are lizards found on all continents, except Antarctica. Some use camouflage to hide from predators and prey.

 Fish swim in all Earth's seas. Several species dwell in forests of kelp—a kind of seaweed that can grow taller than 10-story buildings.

 Rats are rodents that thrive in every country on Earth. Many make their homes in buildings, old and new.

 Ptarmigans are grouse found in North America, Europe, and northern Asia. They have a brown coat in summer and a white coat in winter.

 Yucca moths are insects that pollinate the yucca plants of Mexico and southwestern United States. The larvae feed only on the seeds of these plants.

Text © Diane Swanson 2002
02 03 04 05 06 5 4 3 2 1

All rights reserved. No part of this book may be reproduced, stored in a retrieval system, or transmitted in any form or
by any means without the prior written permission of the publisher or, in the case of photocopying or other reprographic
copying, a license from CANCOPY (Canadian Copyright Licensing Agency), Toronto, Ontario.

Greystone Books
A division of Douglas & McIntyre Ltd.
2323 Quebec Street, Suite 201
Vancouver, British Columbia V5T 4S7
www.greystonebooks.com

National Library Cataloguing in Publication Data
Swanson, Diane, 1944-
   Animals can be hard to see

   ISBN 1-55054-901-4 (bound).—ISBN 1-55054-905-7 (pbk.)
   1. Camouflage (Biology)—Juvenile literature. 2. Color of animals—
   Juvenile literature. I. Title.
QL767.S92 2002   j591.472   C2002-911037-5

Library of Congress Cataloging information is available.

Packaged by House of Words for Greystone Books
Editing by Elizabeth McLean
Cover and interior design by Rose Cowles
Cover photograph by T. Davis/First Light
Photo credits: p. i T. Davis/First Light; p. ii (clockwise from top) B. Fischer/First Light, James Stanfield/First Light,
First Light; p. 2 B. Fischer/First Light; p. 4 Norbert Rosing/First Light; p. 6 First Light; p. 8 James Stanfield/First Light;
p. 10 Darlyne Murawski/First Light; p. 12 First Light; p. 14 T. Davis/First Light; p. 16 First Light; p. 18 First Light

Printed and bound in Hong Kong

A very special note of thanks goes to Dr. Alison Preece, Faculty of Education, University of Victoria, for her guidance
and encouragement in the development of this series.

The publisher gratefully acknowledges the support of the Canada Council for the Arts and of the British Columbia Ministry
of Tourism, Small Business and Culture. The publisher also acknowledges the financial support of the Government of Canada
through the Book Publishing Industry Development Program (BPIDP).